THE FRESH CODER

ADEEB TAHIR

Made with ♥ on the Notion Press Platform
www.notionpress.com

To my parents

Contents

Preface

This was initially just a bunch of raw notes I made, addressed to myself, at the end of each day from my daily experiences as a software engineer. Gradually I started thinking that I can't be the only one who's anxious about my career as a fresher just entering or stepping into the corporate world of enterprise programming. So I made a monthly mini weekend task out of it where on the last Sunday of each month, I would collect all my notes and organize them into something more structured that could pass as chapters of a book. Over due course of time I figured, through my own conversations with my parents, that some of these worries and anxieties are not limited to freshers but also parents of freshers. So I've tried to put in text some of the most common thoughts that were on my mind as well as a few experiences of mine to help give context to the topics.

Of course, **all of the written views, opinions and suggestions expressed in this book are mine and not to be associated with any organization.**

Acknowledgements

I'd like to thank my family who've made many sacrifices and efforts to help me reach where I am today. I also extend my gratitude to all the peers, leads and mentors I've had the pleasure of spending time with and working alongside, whose contributions have been truly invaluable.

CHAPTER ONE

Breaking Down The Wall

If you're a fresher, like I was four years ago, just starting out your software development journey with a million questions of how things are going to pan out, I'm glad you picked this book as I'll try my best to demystify this space over the next eleven chapters, hopefully putting most of your doubts to rest!

Firstly, congratulations on choosing software development as a career path! Contrary to popular belief, software development is a highly creative field in many aspects.

So, I'm sure you too would've sat in numerous interviews and noticed varying job titles for the same set of technical specifications. You may have seen 'Application Developer' in some places, 'Software Developer', 'Software Engineer' and even a few hybrid terms such as 'Software Development Engineer' used in other places.

My two cents on this variation in terminologies is they really can be used interchangeably as a matter of preference.

On examining the term usage trend line[1] for the past ten years (See Fig.1), however, we see the preference of having 'Engineer' in your title has gone up a fair bit, perhaps it being more synonymous with the entire software process from inception to delivery could be one reason as opposed to 'Developer' being synonymous with only the coding aspect of the career.

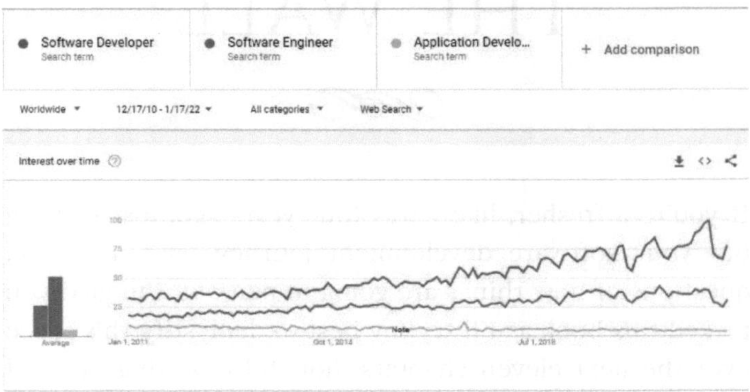

Figure 1 : Software Designation Trend Line

From experience, I just feel the title doesn't matter as long as the technical role specifications are what drive you to wake up excited for!

I named this chapter 'Breaking Down the Wall' as I feel it's the perfect way to start, by breaking down the wall of doubt and I'm sure all freshers have a couple of doubts as they embark on their software journey.

This chapter is to break down how the topics in the book are divided. As a fresher, you may have doubts such as:

"Are the daily challenges I will be working on going to be around the same difficulty as my interview?"

"Should I do another crash course on advanced data structures and algorithms?"

"How do I pick up my project quickly and start excelling at it?"

"Will work let me continue enjoying the other things I do in life?" and many more...

I've organized my book into eleven chapters covering a fair breadth of question categories. Chapter 2 is all about breaking some problem solving myths that you may have seen/heard before. I also show you how you can try to semi-automate a lot of mundane stuff which if you do early enough, saves/creates a huge buffer for you later on!

In Chapter 3, I show you how to set your goals for the year and how they work in a corporate setting.

Later in Chapter 4, we will see how to get rid of pre-project jitters and step into it where I'll talk about everything you can do to fully embrace changes and rotations.

In Chapters 5-9, we look at how the job affects our personal lives and how to go about that. This mid-section covers the nitty gritty aspects of the job, the daily/weekly trade-offs we have to make mentally in order to really be at peace with ourselves.

Chapters 10-11 cover yet another really important aspect of how to make the most out of limited time. The Covid-19 pandemic really brought on a massive change in the way we work. Towards the end of my book, I shed some light on its impact, and also cover some pointers on remote work, leave planning and some closing thoughts.

CHAPTER TWO

Problem Solving - Debunked

If you're stepping into the software corporate ring for the first time, you may have a few doubts on the nature of problem solving involved. Is it going to be the same as when I interviewed at the company? Will I only get a short window to solve new problems before I move on to others? Is it okay if I'm not able to solve a problem? Will getting stuck for too long on something affect my evaluations? Am I only going to work on one problem at a time?

Speaking from personal experience, I can confirm the environment you experienced during your interview and the actual work environment are miles apart. They couldn't be further apart. One of the traits that recruiters look for in potential candidates is the ability to quickly find observable/derivable patterns in the presented contexts/questions, such that when they come up with solutions, they not only answer the question at hand, but also explain why the solution works, i.e. the ability to correlate the various concepts and properties in data structures/ algorithms (DSA) to the context and present a solution that does the job within reasonable space and time complexity.

Whether the problem is complex or trivial is of less importance. The only thing that matters during an interview is to not give up and keep going at the problems, approaching them with different angles.

The interview room and your work desk do share the similarity that you create solutions for problems in a reasonable time window.

At work, the process of deriving the solutions to the problems you'll work on is a different ball game in terms of scale or magnitude. You may be required to break out of your comfort zone and interact with dozens of stakeholders/dependent teams/individuals in order to truly construct an optimal solution. Again, I'd say that this optimality is relative owing to the several factors at play such as design limitations, technical limitations, policies, data dependencies etc.

You may have to stay online at unearthly hours to get the information you need... I'm just kidding on this one! Thank goodness we have email huh?

So the questions that immediately come to mind are: How are problems solved at the corporate scale?

Before I answer this non-trivial question, think back to when I said "...the process of deriving the solutions to the problems you'll work on is a different ball game in terms of scale or magnitude". In a corporate setting, since the requirements are constantly evolving and pertaining to the specific business units within the organization, usually there is going to be someone that understands all the business jargon really well. This person is the business analyst or BA in short. They are responsible for strategically aggregating all of the demands from business executives and bringing forth these new requirements/improvements to the development team.

Every project needs a working methodology. This is the framework or process you will use to ship features to the end user. Agile Scrum[2] is one of the most widely used methodologies in the industry today. In Scrum, teams commit themselves to shipping software to the end user at the end of predefined cyclic units of time called 'sprints' which are essentially little time boxes that last anywhere from 2-4 weeks usually.

To keep it simple, there is a product backlog which contains all the items to be worked on (new features, improvements, tasks, bug-fixes etc.). Prior to each sprint (usually towards the end of the previous sprint), the team gets together and plans the work items for the next sprint.

Depending on developer bandwidth for the particular sprint, they'll be assigned N items to work on. I suppose this answers the question "Am I only going to work on one task at a time?"

Jira is one popular software used to track sprint work items and something I've been using for a long time now.

Although Scrum is widely used, it's not the only system for managing work items. Another methodology is Kanban which also like Scrum aims to improve the quality of code shipped to the end user. However, there are a couple of differences. In Kanban, you don't have the pre-defined pockets of time present in Scrum. Kanban follows a 'cap the work-in-progress' model which is all about reducing the time to delivery for a project. With this model, changes can be shipped continuously and don't have to wait for any predefined pockets of time. Changes can happen anytime unlike Scrum where an effort is made to not make any new changes during an active sprint.

Is it okay if I'm not able to solve a problem? It's not possible for any single individual to know everything about everything. Of course there are going to be times where you will get stuck. That is, however, the beauty of working in a team with different individuals who all harbour varying skillsets but collectively complete each other's weaknesses. So it's okay to get stuck but it's not okay to stay stuck. Just reach out to any of your team members and simply ask for help. In most cases they will be more than happy to help you out. Pulling each other up creates a robust ecosystem at work which helps you deliver product more efficiently.

Your team is NOT going to assign you a hundred tasks right at the get-go. You'll start out with one or two easy tasks which will help you gain exposure of the developer environment. Once you get comfortable, you'll notice your workload gradually increase but it won't be something you can't handle.

During your interview, you would've been tested vigorously on data structures and algorithms and your ability to recall the code for said algorithms. However, at work you won't be coding these algorithms from scratch. In the sense, why reinvent the wheel? You'd most likely be using libraries which already have these algorithms implemented, and quite optimally too! What you will be doing, however, is collaborating with your team and designing solutions which include choosing the right data structures, algorithms, file management strategies, database decisions etc.

One of my favourite sharks on Shark Tank, Mark Cuban, often says "The one thing you cannot buy is time. Time is your most valuable asset..." and I wholeheartedly agree with this. So two things I learnt and started following pretty early on is:

1. **AUTOMATE EVERYTHING YOU CAN**
2. **STREAMLINE EVERYTHING YOU CAN**

There are no buts and ifs, you just ought to do it, period! You need to actively be on the lookout for processes you do daily that involve some manual effort, or are irksome in any manner whatsoever and just find ways to automate them.

Let me give you three very simple examples of making daily tasks easier. Now, of course, I'm not going to go into any specific business use case, which would vary for everyone depending on their project. I will present trivial examples. The idea being that the same concept can be applied to bigger processes.

Example 1: Let's say I know my team uses JIRA to track sprint items and I also know it's a real pain to open the JIRA sprint board, scroll all the way down to my name and open a specific task link that opens in a new tab that has some data I'd like to reference frequently while working on that item. Bookmarking the page wouldn't help in this case as if I bookmark hundreds of JIRA items, I'd again have to manually hunt for the specific bookmark amongst several others which would again waste time.

My solution is to semi-automate (if not automate) this such that I can instantly view the data I need for a specific JIRA item. Let's assume I'm working on a Windows PC. I create a simple batch file and name it 'jira.bat' which takes a single argument, the JIRA number. If no argument is provided, it just opens the main JIRA dashboard where I can see all the tasks assigned. If a number is provided, it takes me to the specific JIRA task details page.

```
@echo off
set baseUrl="https://jiraDashboardUrl/projectCode"
IF "%~1" == "" GOTO HOMEPAGE

start chrome %baseUrl%/%1%
GOTO FINISH

:HOMEPAGE
start chrome %baseUrl%

:FINISH
exit
```

jira.bat

Example 2: I love puzzles. One of my hobbies is solving competitive programming questions on sites such as codeforces. I also maintain a private GitHub repository where I store my solutions to all the problems I solve. Each solution is stored in its own folder with the same name as the question. For instance, I would store the solution to question 568A in a folder named '568A' and in a file called '568ASol.cpp'. Every solution file has some common code (boilerplate code) for defining constants and methods for input retrieval, type acronyms etc. which are copied from boilerplate.cpp which I maintain elsewhere.

To answer a new problem, I would earlier have to manually create a new folder for the solution, copy the boilerplate contents into that and open the file via my editor of choice VSCode. I automated this process by writing a script 'gen.bat'. Now I can just run "gen 568A" in cmd!

```
@echo off
IF "%~1%" == "" GOTO NO_ARG

set oname=%1
set basePath="F:\codingMisc\CppProjects\codeforces-problems"
mkdir %basePath%\%oname%
copy /y F:\devtools\boilerplate.cpp %basePath%\%oname%\%oname%Sol.cpp
start code %basePath%\%oname%\%oname%Sol.cpp
GOTO FINISH

:NO_ARG
print "No problem Number provided...Exiting"

:FINISH
exit
```

gen.bat

Example 3: One of the common practices most teams follow while preparing SQL scripts for an upcoming production release is preparing a set of rollback scripts anticipating the event that something fails during the release which would require us to roll back the database state to the previous configs. If the config rollbacks are simple and straightforward and follow this model: "Current release' rollback is the immediate previous release' config deployment script" you can easily automate the prep for this.

This is just an extension of the previous example and is all about automating file operations. In this scenario, you would ideally just need to copy the previous release' deployment SQL scripts and paste them in the 'rollback' folder of the current release path. You can call the script 'prep-rb.bat'. You can do something similar as an exercise to get used to writing scripts.

Since these scripts all serve as helpers to the developer, I just call them 'devtools' so I recommend just aggregating all your helper scripts into a single folder called 'devtools' somewhere on your PC. Let's say you place them at this path "C: \devtools"

Now all you need to do is make them available in the main system path for your account. If you're on a Windows PC, you can do this by following the below steps:

Step 1: Hit the search icon on your taskbar and search for 'environment'

Step 2: Select 'edit the environment variables for your account' option under settings

Step 3: Click the 'Path' variable and click 'Edit'

Step 4: Add your devtools path to the list here (i.e. "C: \devtools")

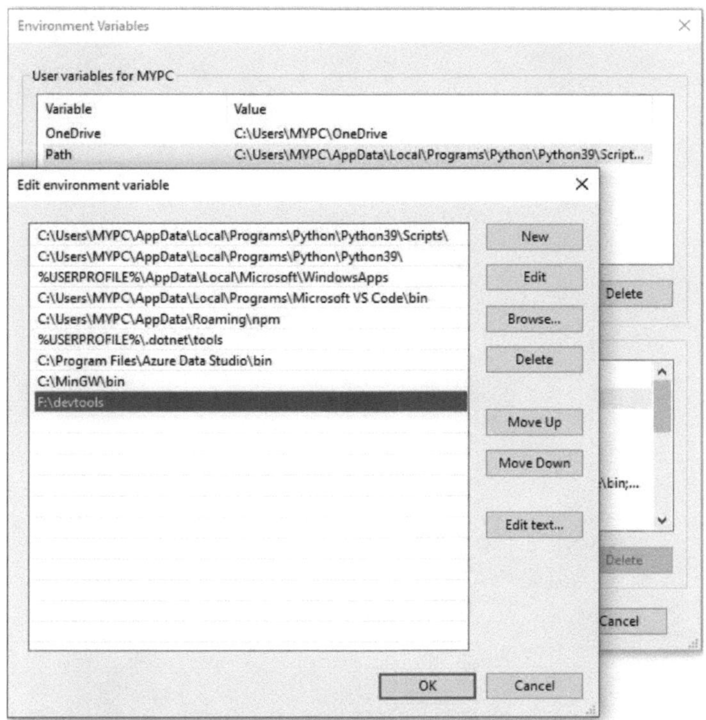

CHAPTER THREE

SETTING GOALS

Every employee be it a fresher or veteran has to come up with and set their goals for the coming year. Usually there is some online portal where you'd submit them on. There are also, to a certain extent, some pointers provided by both team leads as well as the HR teams that oversee your business unit.

The main idea of having goals is to set milestones for yourself along the year to measure how effectively you spend your year. Goals can be short term, mid-term or even long term. An important aspect of setting goals is that you need to ensure that the goal you set also aligns with the direction the business is moving in. That ensures that progress is not one sided and is a win-win situation for both the business as well as you personally/professionally.

Let's say the business unit or function you work in has a milestone of shifting its services from physical nodes to cloud services and you aren't too savvy with the cloud. In this case, a goal like "Learn about cloud and migrate [XYZ] service to [ABC] test cloud environment by July 20XX" is fantastic as it's perfectly in sync with the business as well as your technical aspirations.

Putting a clock on your goals is very important as it helps you truly measure how close or far you've reached later.

While there aren't any universal standards on how goals are set, there are certainly very highly efficient mental goal models that can be followed to yield great goals.

One such model you can keep in mind when setting your goals is ensure that they are SMART[3]. I learnt this model three months into my first job and it just blew me away by how simple yet effective it is.

S.M.A.R.T is an acronym that stands for:

- **S**pecific
- **M**easurable
- **A**chievable
- **R**elevant
- **T**ime Bound

Let's go through each of these in a little more detail.

Specific: When drafting your goals for the year, you need to ask yourself: What am I trying to accomplish? Am I going to be directly responsible for this? Are there any concrete steps I can follow in order to achieve it? If you answer these questions while framing your goal, without a doubt, your goal will become specific.

For example you could draft a goal that goes along the lines of "Reduce the number of weekly support queries related to [XYZ] logic by creating a properly documented info page and making it available on [ABC] path"

This goal is specifically targeted at reducing [XYZ] logic related support queries. You will achieve that by specifically creating a documentation and making it available on [ABC] path

Measurable: How will you know when you've achieved your goal? Is there any metric or quantifiable number you have in place that can help assess your progress? Answering this while framing your goal makes it measurable. An example of this would be extending the same goal we defined earlier and adding a quantifiable metric:

"Reduce, by 50%, the number of weekly support queries related to [XYZ] logic by creating a properly documented info page and making it available on [ABC] path"

The goal now becomes specific and measurable. To measure the progress, all you do is take the total mails related to [XYZ] logic and divide that by the average number of weekly mails you received before implementing the change.

Achievable: It's nice to dream big but at the end of the day, you need to see to it that each action you make towards the goal closes the distance by a reasonable amount. It should be tangible and within the realm of achievability. If you were working on a long term project for an interactive bot, you can't keep a goal such as "I'm going to create a replica of Jarvis from IronMan by this fall..." It's just unrealistic and puts you in a pickle later on.

What you could do, however, is specify the completion of a sub-module for the bot within the same time frame. That makes more sense.

Relevant: All the great goals you set for the year won't matter if they aren't relevant to the project you're working on, to the business unit/function you belong to.

Let's say you work in a product development team that ships over the air updates for robotic kitchen equipment lines and you set a goal such as "Get certified in [XYZ], a course on astrophysics by passing the [ABC] exam scheduled this September". Now this goal is specific, measurable and achievable but while you may personally be interested in learning about [XYZ] and it may be a really cool subject, it has no relation with your current business function's goals. It's better to keep those to yourself and work on them over the weekends or on your own personal spare time.

Time Bound: Whenever you set a goal, put a cap on when you want to achieve it by. This puts a clock on your goal and drives you to make reasonable decisions in favour of achieving the target. We could redefine our earlier goal by saying:

"Reduce, by 50%, the number of weekly support queries related to [XYZ] logic by creating a properly documented info page and making it available on [ABC] path by October 1st 20XX"

Now this goal is complete. It is specifically targeted at reducing support queries related to [XYZ] logic and defines how it can be accomplished. It is quantifiable by providing a way of testing its progress (50% reduction). It is definitely achievable and within the realm of reality. It is relevant to the business as which business wouldn't want to reduce support queries. It is time bound and has a clock capping at Oct 1st of 20XX.

CHAPTER FOUR

Stepping Into Projects

When I was in my final year at university, after I cleared all my interviews, I had a pretty long wait before I joined my first job. My final semester exams finished sometime in March/April while my job started only towards the end of July. So, effectively, I was sitting at home for just about three whole months.

I got the jitters of my life when my 'holiday' began. For four days straight, I could only think of what-if scenarios in my head. I had never worked in a professional environment before, apart from a short internship I did previously. Most of the people I knew had already joined their new roles in different companies while I was just that unemployed guy who stays at home. I honestly freaked out. I didn't know whether I should do some courses and prepare some material prior to joining the job. After the fourth day of utter mental anguish, I made a decision that shaped the rest of my three month holiday.

I thought to myself "I've already done the hard part, cleared the interview, passed my semester exams and now I finally have some time for ME!"

So for the next three months until I joined my job, I split my days into two parts: 7:30AM – 10:30AM and 10:30AM – 10:30PM. I started each day by solving a few random coding problems (you don't have to do this, I just did it as I personally love puzzles and it's one of my hobbies) and then from 10:30AM – 10:30PM, I binged my favourite TV shows and anime. I will never regret re-watching all 291 episodes of Dragon Ball Z, all 200 episodes of Naruto, all 500 episodes of Naruto Shippuden, all 366 episodes of Bleach and reading over 800 chapters of the One Piece manga!

Looking back today, I truly agree that it was one of the best decisions ever. Once you join the workforce, rarely will you get the opportunity to take holidays longer than 2 weeks. Three months is out of the question. So when you get a little break before you join your next project, or before you join your first project, make the most of it and do enjoy your personal and family time.

When you join a new project, everything is different naturally. The work environment, the people, perhaps the business domain in case you are switching paths. It can seem daunting but you really don't have anything to worry about if you find the answers/work on the below five KEY tasks. Finding answers at random times and in random orders will make you take ages to get comfortable with the project. So let me save you some time and list down the KEY things you absolutely need to spend time on and nail:

- Understand the people and their skillsets
- Understand the project architecture and its boundaries
- Understand the business domain and how it correlates with the technological framework

- Understand how to debug the services you'll be working on
- Understand the documented protocols for handling day to day support queries and incident management in general
- Understand the release management process

Apart from these, there are a few other less significant aspects, which I may just leave a short note about at the end of this chapter. If you're efficiently able to handle the above, you'll get super comfortable with your project. Let's go through these KEY elements in more detail.

Understanding people and their skillsets: Every team comprises a unique set of people who have their own distinct personalities. Your first job is to get to know each of them professionally as its going to really help you in the long run.

Every project exists because of some synergy between business, tech and management.

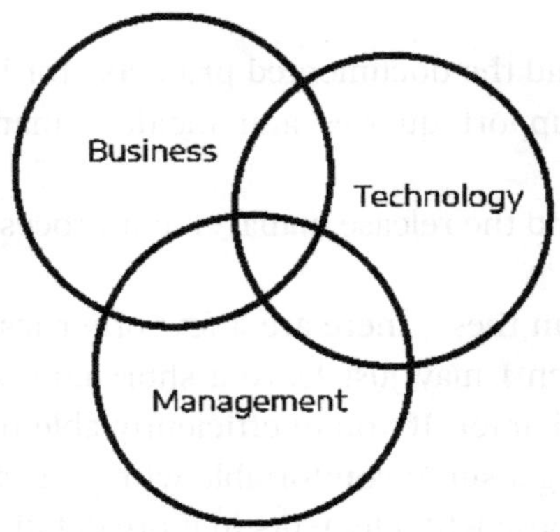

So, one of your first jobs is to get to know everyone. There may be some excellent coders, some excellent business minds, some excellent testers, some absolute all-stars but you won't come to know that by keeping to yourself. Reach out to every member of the team, whether they're from management, business or the tech side and just have a chat. It could be anything, talk about your hobbies, how they got into this career or any other appropriate workplace conversation.

Make a mini goal for the first week if you have to! At the end of week 1, if you can make a mental map that addresses most of the below setup, you're in a pretty good place.

"[ABC] is great at UI and Front-End related stuff"

"[XYZ] is really good at server side matters"

"[DEF] can help me understand the business"

"[PQR] handles the QA side"

"[TUV] is a key contact from the support team"

Understand the project architecture and its boundaries: Once you get a sense of who is who on the team, the next step is to get a feel for the project architecture. This is a very critical step, so ask a million questions when the seniors take KT (knowledge transfer) sessions for you. It doesn't matter if you don't understand something. Ask questions repeatedly until you do. I only tell you this because understanding how your application operates is very important and will help you while you debug its services later on.

It is sufficient if you can mentally map all the services and their dependencies, how they are connected and what is the nature of data they consume, where the services source their data from, where do the services process and send their data to and in what format.

A very popular industrial pattern is microservices following the MVC design where model, view and controller are separated based on duty. JSON and XML are pretty common data interchange formats when it comes to REST enabled services.

So pay close attention to what are the different data structures your application uses, where it sources data from, how it processes the data received and how it transmits the responses. Depending on the nature of the component and nature of data consumed, your service could be using a variety of messaging middleware. If all services are REST enabled, API calls may suffice. You could also use an EMS provider like Tibco EMS or even IBM MQ for messaging. If the data being consumed is huge and in a stream, you may notice the usage of Kafka. Wherever time SLA's need to be met, I often see a caching mechanism in place. This could involve a cache manager like Gemfire.

So it would be a good idea to get the crux of your project architecture. Make a list of all the environment specifications like its software, hardware, caching mechanisms, messaging middleware, front-end frameworks, libraries etc. used and read up on all the tools you are unfamiliar with.

Understand the business domain and how it correlates with the technological framework: Before you jump into the code base, it would immensely help if you took a primer on the business domain that your application helps provide services for/supports/deals with.

Business and technology are intertwined. Without business, there is no compelling context for developing tech and without advancements in tech, there can be no leaps in business capabilities. Get a hold of your seniors, managers and preferably the BA assigned to your project. They will be able to help you navigate and straighten out some unclear concepts you have regarding the parent business your application serves under.

Without understanding the crux of the business, it gets really hard to appreciate the code that drives it. Not every business is made to be learnt easily. That is true. Some businesses are intrinsically much harder to pick up. As a developer, we'll perhaps find it easier to navigate an e-commerce business as opposed to a financial services business.

So it really is a mental trade off when you decide to join a business. Is the time spent (or sweat equity as I like to call it) on learning the business justifiable? If you just want to code and cash out each month, there are several easy businesses to learn. If you want a challenge, there certainly are complex businesses that will eat your head while you pursue comprehending them! My advice on that front would be to just choose wisely. If you find your daily routine strained, ask yourself if it's really what you want in the long run.

Understand how to debug the services you'll be working on: Now that you have a basic foundation of the business domain and project architecture, you can dive into the nitty gritty part of service debugging.

This is where your true understanding of the project comes into play. If you are able to successfully debug a few services and ship some production grade code to the end user, YAY! You did it. Keep at it.

It's really important to catch a colleague and ask them to show you how to debug all the services once. That will show you what arguments the services take, how they should be debugged. I remember I was debugging some services in a painstakingly long way until a senior showed me a cool and easy way to do it. So in short, if you find a decent way to do something and it works, find a better way to do it!

Understand the documented protocols for handling day to day support queries and incident management in general: In most cases, you'll find yourself debugging existing code instead of coding new things. So it's really important to get familiar with the debug environment and learn how to handle application queries raised by the support teams and other business stakeholders.

Most projects usually have their online stores where they host all their documentation. I would suggest spending some time there when you're just starting out with it to understand more intricacies of the application, more than what's possibly covered in the KT sessions. It's of course impossible to cover everything about the application in a short 30 minute session. Nowadays, codebases run anywhere from a couple hundred thousand to millions of lines of code.

This is the reason why so many practitioners in the industry highly recommend writing clean and optimal code right from the start. It's more expensive to clean up buggy code in production than it is to rectify it in test environments.

You can observe your team's mailbox for a few weeks and see how your colleagues respond to the mails from support. You can learn an awful lot just from going through those responses. You get an idea of who are the major players for any issue, who to direct queries to, how to respond to certain types of messages etc.

Every company follows a well-documented system of incident management. If they didn't, it'd be utter chaos. So ask your colleagues for a sample incident number for any issue and go through how the tickets were raised, how teams collaborate while solving incidents and how the central incident ticket platform works. You'll require this knowledge later on when you are assigned some tasks for which you need to raise tickets to resolve.

Understand the release management process: There is a whole lot of effort that goes into shipping code from your release branch to production. Understanding the intricacies of your applications release process can shed some light on its inherent architectural complexity.

Join the release coordinator for any production release of your application and observe first-hand what they do to deploy the app on production servers. Production preparation starts several days prior to release day or D-day (deployment day).

You'd notice your team preparing a document called the release document or release note which consists of all the features being shipped in the coming release. Make note of all the deployment tools being used and how each production release follows a systematic process which ensures its success. The production environment is a highly controlled environment and every effort is made to keep it stable at all cost. Downtimes are seriously chased as they could potentially cause loss of revenue for the business.

These were the six KEY points of focus that if you spend ample time on, you'll do great! Once you complete the above areas of focus, it's time to put yourself out there and really test yourself. You've observed your colleagues handle certain queries and issues, now can you do the same when they aren't around?

Take any query that you see one of your colleagues frequently handles, and offer to take it off their plate for a week. If you are able to do that, there is no other better proof that you really have blended into the project quite well.

Over the past few years I've come across several comments online that say, not exactly verbatim but I'm paraphrasing a whole bunch of them, "Coding is an introverted career path..." and to this I would reply "Not at all! It's completely up to the developer what kind of career they want to create".

Within programming careers, we have several distinctions. Some projects emphasise greater scope for individual contribution which is great for people who like to keep to themselves and have introverted personalities. On the other hand, you also have many projects where large scale collaboration is involved on a daily basis, which is perfect for extroverted personalities. Recruiters wouldn't hesitate to work together with candidates in order to get them into a project that's best suited for them.

CHAPTER FIVE

Finding Your Happy Place

I felt now is a great time to bring up an important topic which addresses the below question if you've ever had it:

"Will work let me continue enjoying the other things I do in life?"

The answer is nothing can stop you from truly doing something except yourself. If you feel your work is eating up your personal time and space, it's because you are allowing it eat into your personal time and space. If you fail at clearly demarcating the boundary between your work and personal life, things such as crossovers will undoubtedly happen. It won't be a matter of if, rather a matter of when.

An easy question you can ask yourself immediately is what's more important, your job or your mental and physical well-being? My answer has and always will be the latter. While it's really important to focus and do well in your job, you should NEVER EVER compromise on your mental and physical well-being.

There used to be a time where I used to leave my house at 7:00 AM in the morning and return only at 10:30/11:00

PM at night as my office was a 1.5 hour (single-way) drive away from home. When I returned home daily, I just had enough time to have dinner, get changed and go to bed. The routine repeated again the next morning where I'd be out the house by 7:00 AM.

This went on for quite a while, around 3 months if I remember right. I was really exhausted, depressed, had no time for myself, wasn't able to spend much time with my family either. I absolutely hated it.

Spending over ten hours of my day at work daily resulted in me understanding my job really well; I was great at it but it came at the cost of my personal mental peace. I wasn't happy. What started out as enthusiasm soon brought me misery.

I finally snapped one day and decided to start leaving work two hours earlier each day. I came in really early each day so leaving two hours earlier than usual meant that I still did my daily eight hour minimums. These two new hours that I now had to spare when I came home were like fresh breaths of oxygen. I could now eat my dinner slowly without rushing, had time to talk to my family and even squeeze in a little reading time. I found myself getting happy again.

Now just because I gave my personal example above, doesn't mean I expect you to extrapolate it and work lesser hours claiming you're unhappy working even the minimum hours expected. If you find yourself dreading coding or being around code for even eight hours a day, you really should rethink your career. This may not be the right one for you.

The purpose of the above example is to emphasize that you need to take care of your physical and mental well-being and make time for yourself and your family. At the end of the day when it's time to clock out of work, it may seem tempting to respond to 'just one more' mail and then sign off. I say "If it's not critical and has an ample time frame for response, it can wait!"

You have TWO days each week which you can devote to yourself and your family. If you find yourself working on weekends, it's honestly sad. Unless there is some production outage or prior commitment that requires your attention over the weekend, don't log into your work station.

Since you're spending over 40 hours a week staring at the computer screen, its ideal to find non-digital means of entertainment on the weekends. A sport such as table tennis or basketball does wonders. I personally enjoy learning musical instruments. I play the guitar, keyboard and recently purchased a ukulele. It ships next week so can't wait to rock out on that mini stringed instrument.

CHAPTER SIX

Like A Snowball

Now that we've covered some serious work stuff, I'll throw in a story from my past. It's FLASHBACK TIME!

I was an extremely introverted kid, and still am, and found it incredibly hard to make new friends when my environment changed. At any point of time in my life, I could literally count, on my hand, the friends I had. That was fine by me ...really! I was really happy too. Knowing and staying in touch with less than ten friends would make me really satisfied.

I left Dubai and headed to Chennai for my high school. I couldn't have dreaded the time I left more because I had to leave behind friends I'd known for over ten years and start from scratch in a place I'd only visited a couple of times before during my school vacations. The fact I didn't know Tamil at the time didn't do me any favours either.

To give some more context to the story, due to some mystical magical reasons, my family decided to buy a house in the MIDDLE OF NOWHERE, in a small village that ended up being OVER 27 KILOMETERS away from my then new school. I used to complaint about this to my mom every single day for two years but staying away from the city actually helped me in ways you cannot imagine.

So my first day at high school was just your average day until it wasn't. My first memory of high school is entering the twelfth grade classroom thinking it was my eleventh grade room and sitting there like a vase in the corner until a senior reached out.

I rushed to the chemistry lab on the ground floor which was where my actual eleventh grade peers were at.

However, thank you my fellow senior who saved this introvert from further embarrassment!

Cut to the chemistry lab, where my classmates are working on our beloved high school 'salt analysis' experiment. I got partnered with this curly haired, happy go-lucky and extremely extroverted stranger. Let's call him Stark, which obviously isn't his real name for privacy reasons.

I thought I was done for. He kept probing me, breaking down the communication wall with each question, little by little. Literally an introvert's worst nightmare. Interestingly, we became great friends in school.

Although I was this introverted kid, would you believe I've actual won competitions for public speaking in English and Hindi? Would you also believe I was part of my high school debate team? At the time, I always thought I was lucky but looking back I've come to realize that luck too is something your active efforts or decisions have a role in shaping.

My handwriting used to be pretty horrible and my family spared no effort whatsoever in reminding me of the same. I remember once, they said it was akin to a pen tied to the feet of a crazy chicken running around the field. While I couldn't change that no matter what I tried, I made it my life's mission to master the art of speech and comprehension. If you can't write neatly, may as well rock the speaking and listening part right? I feel the conscious efforts I made little by little had a snowball effect towards the end which somewhat helped reduce my introverted nature, but not completely, around new people and surroundings. So yeah, it's been about ten years now.

Are you wondering what happened to Stark? Well, he's my best friend and we attended the same college and even worked together! So if you've been paying close attention, you probably picked up the secret to getting by in work if you're more of an introvert: Drag your best friend to accompany you till the end of your career... KIDDING!

Jokes aside, the point of the story was to emphasize that constant periodic micro efforts collectively aggregate over time to produce macro results. I don't believe that luck is a matter of chance, it's the increase in likelihood of a favourable outcome due to the micro efforts we systematically make over a period of time akin to a snowball that rolls down a hill and collects all the little objects along the way to yield a massive snowball.

CHAPTER SEVEN

TUTORIAL HELL

We're now halfway through my book. I hope you're enjoying it as much as I did writing it. For this chapter, I decided to talk about something that's very near and dear to my heart, "tutorials".

I personally believe there is nobody on Earth that consumes, by volume, video tutorial content more aggressively than software developers. Almost every single day, there is something new in the software scene. We consume tutorials for data structures and algorithms, frameworks and tools, installation guides and a million other things. Just the other day I did a simple web search (as a guest user on YouTube, else you will get personalized recommendations which adds a bias) for the key word 'tutorial' without any context and the top results contained:

- Minecraft
- More Minecraft
- Python
- Java Programming

We've done it people! We've dominated the tutorial space and made it so saturated that even if we didn't give context to the word 'tutorial', we'd get search results related to programming.

I reckon everybody and their neighbour has their own programming tutorial online, which begs the question "How do you create a learning pathway with so many tutorials online?"

Also how do you avoid falling prey to the endless cycle of tutorials? I'll admit that I too have fallen victim to this cycle of tutorials for a while when I was just starting out coding in eleventh grade and it almost ate me alive.

For example, let's say you see a tutorial called "Build [ABC] using React, MySQL etc." that contains a playlist of 5 videos. Later you see a similar tutorial by another creator which has 25 videos. So you think to yourself "Did I get the short end of the stick with the earlier playlist? Have I missed a bunch of core concepts that I should know?" and this mental loop deepens and gets worse with every new playlist you see which contains similar content and varying number of videos.

It's easier to pick 2-3 uploaders with a good track record and follow their content to learn whatever it is you're learning. And later on a need-to-know basis, you could always look up videos on the go.

I prefer looking at the already available forums and extremely well written documentation out there which is an excellent source to start on new tools.

Another really great source of learning material is your own company project's source code. Drill down and get to the nitty gritty details of implementation. That will give you a pretty good idea of how scalable code is written on an enterprise wide level.

Moreover, most companies have their own knowledge base when it comes to tool and framework learning for which they would provide in-house training from seasoned veterans and your own seniors or even arrange for corporate training initiatives. They would already have the partnerships in place with online education providers that you could fully utilize to your advantage.

Employers invest a lot into the technical knowledge of their employees, so before you waste money purchasing a course online to understand something at work, see if you can arrange for KTs in-house or explore if there are already existing courses available within your organization that could help you learn the same.

It might be tempting to pick up the new framework that appears every 2-3 months, but before you decide to invest your time on them, consider that you don't want to end up in a situation where you spread yourself too thin!

So the next time you think about cram learning Angular.js, electron.js, Vue.js, Next.js, etc. all at once, first master the root that all these libraries are based off of: JavaScript. Then you can do anything; it becomes very easy to pick up any of the other JS derivatives!

CHAPTER EIGHT

Stress Test

As software engineers, we have a keen eye for finding bugs. Having said that, it would be within reason to assume we're also quick to find things that are irksome in our day.

Things can go sideways really fast if you're not careful. So it's best to mentally push aside any environmental or externally agitating stimuli which could be factors such as an unpleasant commute to work due to traffic or even tiny shaving nicks.

My worst day was when I forgot to check the weather forecast for the day and quickly dashed to work on my scooter. Thirty minutes on the commute and it starts raining heavily. I obviously got drenched. It doesn't stop there as to top it, a reckless bus driver zipped past a red traffic signal and I had muddy water all over my jeans, which brings me to my point earlier that things can go sideways really fast if you're not careful.

Your day belongs to you, so don't let anybody else ruin it. If anything, ruin it yourself... KIDDING!

Either way if you won't ruin it, there are plenty of chances that your code or your compiler will ruin it for you!

Employers are already aware of this possibility of stress and have made efforts to help alleviate the same. Most workplaces have their own game rooms with fully loaded pool table and table tennis table. You can bring your racquet and play sports with your mates!

Depending on the nature if your project, you may not get a chance to have an hour of game time, but doesn't mean you can't reach home and play away in the evenings.

Do try to squeeze in forty five minutes to an hour of high cardio activities daily though, helps you in the long run.

I've attended loads of those live sessions where industry veterans talk about their journey. One excellent pointer from one of those sessions is, and I'm paraphrasing, "If you chase work-life balance in your everyday schedule, you may not get it. However, if you see the larger picture, it'll be there" which is true if you make the periodic micro efforts I spoke about earlier.

CHAPTER NINE

Tech talks, Workshops & Mailboxes

One of the most exciting parts of working in an organization is the plethora of events that are conducted on premises and virtually. They could range from quizzes, technical speaker sessions, product knowledge sessions, business domain workshops, trainings and expos.

The registrations for these events are so wild that the vacant slots disappear if you don't act fast enough. So the next time you see an event that you're personally inclined towards, don't hesitate and register right away. Even if some sudden unavoidable work pops up, your spot isn't going to get wasted due to the waitlists. As soon as you get the mail, register immediately!

Speaking of mail, let's address another important aspect of your programming work life, adequate mailbox management.

If I had to take a guess, I see around five hundred to a thousand new emails daily in my inbox. Now if I didn't have an appropriate folder structure on Outlook (or whichever mail client you use), I'd be tearing the hair out of my head in no time.

Ideally you want some peace of mind and easy navigation for your mails. Go ahead and create the below folders in your mail client, it will save you tons of time and bring a tear to your eye when you realize you skipped going through over four hundred irrelevant mails, and there will be quite a fair share of mail that you'd delete in a heartbeat to save space.

The below eight folders have made my days easier and it could certainly help you too!

- <Team Name>
- <Support Team>
- <System Alerts>
- <Tax Info>
- <Manager>
- <HR Updates>
- <General>
- <ASAP>

I recommend adding an 'ASAP' folder for those items you need to definitely look at. You can add a shortcut that moves urgent mails to this folder for quick reference later on.

CHAPTER TEN

REST

An often overlooked yet incredibly important factor that affects how successfully we go through our work for the day is whether we got an adequate amount of sleep the night before.

In our career path as programmers, it's all the more important to get sufficient sleep as we tend to stare at monitors for extended durations of the day. The net effect of that activity coupled with sleep deprivation provides the micro catalyst that builds up over time to cause red and strained eyes.

In today's digital age, our lifestyle choices for the most part are terribly unhealthy. What do we do when we clock out from work? We close the work stations and immediately fire up our OTT apps that deliver us fresh content we look forward to each day. The problem isn't the fact that we watch our favourite shows or movies, it is we don't give a big enough gap between switching screens.

Let's do some math, say we're glued to the screen 14 hours a day on average, which is not far from the truth to be honest.

In a regular day, we're awake 16 out the 24 hours. So that gives us (16 x 365) or 5840 hours that we're awake in a year.

Let's be really conservative and rule out 25 days in the year and assume we live the caveman life for those 25 days. That leaves us with 340 days to use our gadgets with, so we're on the screen for (340 x 14) or 4760 hours.

We are effectively glued to the screen over 81% of the hours we are awake in a year and this is assuming a moderate amount of sleep, i.e. 8 hours of sleep.

What happens when we decide to play around with these configs and extend our screen time till 3AM in the morning daily? NOTHING GOOD certainly.

I've personally played around with this config and also suffered its consequences. A year and a half into the pandemic, like everyone else, I was working from home. I must've been clocking 15-16 hours a day on the computer minimum. While I fully understood the demerits of prolonged screen time, I continued the prolonged usage and one day noticed the corner of my eye squinting at random intervals. I thought "Okay, today was a long day, I'll be fine tomorrow..." The next day the eye irritation didn't stop. It got worse by the hour and after a few days, the corner of my eyes were sore from me rubbing them repeatedly to get rid of the watery sensation. It got so bad I was literally washing my eyes with cold water every 15-20 minutes which is downright a nuisance and impractical to do if I were working at office or somewhere outside.

I visited the local ophthalmologist and the doctor said I had a bad case of 'dry-eyes'. I found that it's pretty common in the IT industry and was a major complaint during the pandemic. The doctor also told me that fortunately my eyes weren't that far gone yet so they could be treated with simple eye drops and a tablet which was prescribed for about 2 months. However, I hated the whole process of going to the clinic, having dilation drops put on my eyes which semi-blinded me for 4-5 hours and then having my eyes examined. There is not a snowball's chance in hell I'm doing that to myself again.

These last couple of years, the coronavirus pandemic has changed a lot of things. It has to some extent also affected the hours we work. Work hours have become slightly longer, no doubt due to the absence of physical commute and the 'Work-From-Home' (WFH) model. So do take plenty of rest and watch your screen time!

CHAPTER ELEVEN

Working Remotely & Leave Planning

You're still here and reading? I can't thank you enough for sticking all the way through. This is the final chapter of my book and I thought I'd touch base on two important things that developers constantly think about and do. As I mentioned in the last chapter, the coronavirus pandemic has definitely caused a scary chain of cataclysmic operational changes around the globe. This is not just in the software and IT lines but also in almost every business that requires operations at scale to function. The businesses that were able to do the digital pivot strategically succeeded in retaining their customers whereas the physical-retail-only businesses had a major income stream nearly wiped out due to the lockdowns and other regulations.

One of the most notable changes is our working model. Most of us sit at home now and operate remotely. Five months into the covid-19 pandemic, my first mandatory project rotation was due. This meant I had to move into a new team completely virtually, which was a first for me. Whenever I stepped into projects earlier, I met face to face with everyone in person which helped break the ice in a comfortable manner. However this rotation threw that out the window!

Till date, I've yet to meet them all in person. I have definitely interacted with them over video chats but it honestly isn't the same as a real 'in-person' conversation. For a long time I associated their names with voice tones, and after having our first video chat, the association got upgraded and a rectangular video frame got registered as well! Hopefully the pandemic ends soon and normalcy is restored across the globe. It certainly needs it.

On another note, this remote WFH model has absolutely resulted in quite amusing sitting postures, particularly amongst the youth. I've personally experimented with a few and found them hilarious yet comfortable.

Now that we've had a few smiles, I'll leave you with the last topic I want to cover, which is 'leave planning'.

Let's say you have about 30 holidays in a year. How would you go about making the most of them? While still having fun of course! The only right answer is effective leave planning.

I usually prepare a leave chart/table at the start of each year which gives me a rough idea of how I'm going to spend my year allowing ample room for flexibility as I know for a fact that things don't always go out as planned especially if you plan things too far in advance. Having said that, however, you definitely need a rough plan in your head to accommodate scenarios on the fly.

Particularly at the start of your career, it's quite important to work on upskilling yourself every single day and planning your time off strategically to enable you to upskill yourself. Almost three years into my career and I'm still always on the lookout for when is the next free time I will get to read something cool and I try to make micro efforts whenever possible in order to realize a macro effect.

An example would be during work when you're preparing a release branch build of your changes. Let's say you have no other pressing work items or matters that need your attention, fire up your browser and do a little reading on that new tool or framework you want to learn about while the release branch is building.

At the start of each year, I make a spreadsheet with the following contents:

- Skills I want to learn
- Government holidays
- Organization holidays
- Holidays on the weekend
- Upcoming family events
- Prior commitments

Now I use this as a source to prepare an initial leave projection table that contains all the planed leaves I'll be taking for the year along with a description of why I'm taking them.

Once you have this in place, you can update it on the fly as the year progresses. They key thing to remember is don't overwork yourself on the holidays. Also, do save some time for family vacations and a few 'do-nothing' days which are essential to keeping your sanity when things get too hectic. Personally, I try to block a week for December end as that's when most of my family is free to travel.

To summarise, you ought to plan a schedule which:

- Is completely in sync with your work duties
- Allows time for personal rest and relaxation

- Allows time for family events/vacations
- Provides ample opportunity to upskill yourself

Simple enough right? Not quite, it's easier said than done. Truth be told, you won't bring it to fruition unless you actively work on keeping your manager(s), team leads, co-workers and family informed of your plans. This will save you the trouble of finding yourself in difficult situations later on.

Great! This was all I wanted to share with you, for now. I'm sure if you actively work on the things mentioned in the book, your programming career will get a smooth start and you'll do fairly well, I dare say you will absolutely KILL IT at work.

Take care, stay safe and until we meet again... Cheers!

Closing Thoughts

I'd like to firstly thank you all, my readers, who decided to give this author, you've never heard of before, a shot. I've had a lot of joys in my life. Writing this book is definitely up there on the list of memorable experiences in my life. It holds and always will hold a special place within me as it's also the first book I've written. There is no crystal ball that's going to magically show you how your career will pan out, let's get that right. However, we'd be nuts not to believe in the snowball effect right? I've always seen snowballs used in a negative way in speech and writing so I thought of rebranding the cute little snowball! I love the idea of associating micro efforts with little snowballs that aggregate over time to produce macro results. I've tried my best to alleviate common doubts or anxieties freshers (and to a certain degree parents of freshers) may have about their programming journey. I hope this book helped you, even in the smallest way possible!

Cheers,
Adeeb Tahir

References

1. https://trends.google.com/trends/explore?date=2010-12-17 2022-01-17&q=Software Developer,Software Engineer,Application Developer
2. https://www.atlassian.com/agile/kanban/kanban-vs-scrum
3. Doran, G. T. (1981). "There's a S.M.A.R.T. way to write management's goals and objectives". Management Review. 70 (11): 35–36.

Printed by Libri Plureos GmbH in Hamburg, Germany